D1145019

Where In The World Am I?

Mystery Geography Puzzles

Lagoon Books, London

Series Editor: Simon Melhuish
Editor and writer: Heather Dickson
Research: Heather Dickson, Victoria Barber &
Jonathan Bouthémy de Chavières
Page design and layout: Linley Clode
Cover design: Linley Clode

Published by:
LAGOON BOOKS

PO BOX 311, KT2 5QW, UK

ISBN: 1899712410

© LAGOON BOOKS, 1996.

Printed in Singapore.

Where In The World Am I?

Mystery Geography Puzzles

LAGOON
BOOKS

Introduction

This pocket-sized puzzle book is packed full of interesting geographic, historic and socio-economic clues and selected snippets of information to help you decide...

WHERE IN THE WORLD AM I?

With the help of ten clues, in an order of decreasing difficulty, you have to guess which city, country or place is being described on each page.

Anyone who can guess the whereabouts after having read only TWO clues is a geographical genius.

Anyone who can guess the whereabouts after having read only FOUR clues should go to the top of the class.

Anyone who can guess the whereabouts after having read only SIX clues should be applauded.

Anyone who can guess the whereabouts after having read EIGHT clues should get a pat on the back.

Anyone who needs to read all TEN clues to guess the whereabouts should consider investing in an atlas.

Anyone who cannot guess where in the world is being described, should take the next opportunity to buy a round-the-world airplane ticket!

The first clue on every page indicates whether the place being described is a city, a capital city or a country. If it is none of these, then assume it is a state, a dependency, an overseas territory, a river or a mountain etc.

Where in the World Am I? will provide hours of entertainment for the reader but it can also be played by a group. Players take turns to read out the clues, the first person to guess the correct city, country or place wins. Anyone who guesses incorrectly should sit out until someone gets it right and you move onto a new page.

Where in the World Am I? can also be played in teams. One person in each team is nominated to read out the questions, then each team takes turns to ask questions, while the other team guesses. Points 1-10 can be awarded depending on when the correct answer is guessed (1 point would be awarded after the first clue, two after the second and so on). Each team has three chances to guess the whereabouts being described, if the fourth guess is wrong, it is the other team's turn and 12 points are added to the team's score. The winner is the team with the lowest number of points.

Answers are given at the back of the book.
Bon voyage!

No ~ 1

1. This capital city sprawls for 522 square miles.

2. In 1985, a huge earthquake destroyed much of the city and is estimated to have killed more than 2,000 people.

3. In the 1980s, the population of the city was increasing at a rate of 3,000 per day.

4. The city's Metropolitan Cathedral took 250 years to build.

5. The Basilica de Guadelupe houses the country's most important religious painting and is a national shrine.

6. With more than 20 million people living here, this is the second largest population centre in the world.

7. The Plaza of the Constitution is the hub of the city.

8. The Aztec capital Tenochtitlán, once stood here.

9. At one point, it was the most important city in the New World.

10. The Gulf of Mexico is to the east of the city and the Pacific Ocean is to the west.

No ~ 2

This capital city is surrounded by salt lakes, that dry out in the summer then re-fill in autumn, attracting flamingos and herons.

During World War II it was occupied by the Germans for more than a year.

The Island of Kerkenna lies off the coast.

The Bardo Museum has one of the world's largest collections of Roman mosaics.

The port is called La Goulette (The Gullet).

The city's Djama el Zitouna (Mosque of the Olive Tree) was founded in 732 AD.

The city's wealth and importance surpassed that of Cairo between the 13th and 16th centuries.

It is the home of the 'Arab League'.

The ruins of Carthage are a major tourist attraction.

Add the two letters IA to the name of this city and you have the country of which it is the capital.

No ~ 3

1. Only a quarter of the people in this country live in cities or urban conurbations.

2. According to local legend, a prince called Vijaya conquered this land in the 6th century.

3. The two main religions of this country are Buddhism and Hinduism.

4. The country has been described as The Land without Sorrow and The Land of the Hyacinth.

5. Gemstones found here include sapphires, rubies, beryl and topaz.

6. This republic has been ruled in the past by the Dutch, the Portuguese and the British.

7. Tourist destinations include Polonnaruwa and Anuradhapura.

8. The two languages spoken are Sinhalese and Tamil.

9. Violence made it necessary for an Indian peace keeping force to come to this country in 1987.

10. Former names for this island include Serendib and Ceylon.

No ~ 4

The first people to settle in this city were refugees fleeing the Barbarians in the 5th century.

The city's resident population totals 75,000 yet it attracts 9 million visitors a year.

Although a city of ancient art, visitors can catch a glimpse of something more modern at the Peggy Guggenheim Museum.

It is a pedestrian's haven; few cars are allowed in the city centre.

It is in great danger from pollution.

The island of Murano is the centre of the city's glass-making trade.

At the height of its glory in the 15th century, it was known as the Queen of the Adriatic and had no economic rival.

The 16th century architect Andrea Palladio's masterpiece, San Giorgio Maggiore, can be found opposite St Mark's Square.

The Bridge of Sighs leads from the Doges' Palace over a narrow canal to the old prisons.

A Gondola trip up the Grand Canal is a must for every tourist.

1 2 3 4 5 6 7 8 9 10

No ~ 5

Jesuits were expelled from this country in 1767.

Its early history is shrouded in legends and mythology.

Its capital city was made a UNESCO cultural-heritage site in 1978.

When the invading Spanish Conquistadors executed the Inca chief Atalhualpa in 1532, the Inca Empire was in effect destroyed.

Part of the Spanish Vice-Royalty of Peru from the 16th century, this country got its independence in 1822.

The country's main natural resource is oil.

Seviche, made with fish or shellfish soaked in lime juice and served with a spicy sauce made from bitter oranges, is a local speciality.

The Galapagos Islands belong to this country and lie about 600 miles off its coast.

The Andes, the Amazon rain forest and basin and a coast on the Pacific Ocean can all be found in this country.

The country takes its name from the Equator, on which it lies.

No ~ 6

1. This place is one of the ancient Pillars of Hercules.

2. It was once known as Mons Calpe.

3. To the Romans, it marked the end of the world.

4. Its current name is Berber in origin and means 'Tariq's mountain'.

5. It is thought to have been the last refuge of Neanderthal man before his extinction.

6. A colony of Barbary Apes lives here.

7. It is built on a rock, inside of which there are 10 miles of tunnels.

8. The rock is 1,398ft high and made of Jurassic limestone.

9. It is situated only 14 miles from Africa.

10. An overseas territory of the UK, it is joined to Spain by a sandy isthmus.

No ~ 7

This city is a major seaport, serving major mining and agricultural industries.

An earthquake almost destroyed the city in 1906.

It was from the hills to the south of the city that a scout from the Spanish explorer Gaspar de Portocá's expedition first sighted this place in 1769.

The first cable car was invented and used here in 1873.

The corner of Haight and Ashbury was a favourite hippy hang-out in the 1960s.

It is the home of poet Allen Ginzburg.

Alcatraz, Treasure and Yerba Buena lie in the city's bay.

The 49ers play here.

The streets of this city played a major part in a popular American cop drama.

Visitors approach the city from the north via the Golden Gate.

No ~ 8

This capital city is the centre of the country's railway system.

It celebrated its 800th anniversary in 1947.

It boasts more than 2,500 monuments.

The Cathedral of St Basil was commissioned in the mid 16th century to commemorate the conquest of the Tatar Khanate of Kazan.

Under Ivan the Great, it was known as 'New Constantinople'.

Its underground system has to cope with around 9 million passengers a day.

The city's famous citadel was rebuilt in stone in 1367.

It was invaded by Napoleon in 1812.

A vodka and ginger beer drink is named after this city.

When Lenin arrived in 1922, it became the capital of the Union.

No ~ 9

1. This is the oldest and largest city in the country.

2. It was originally called Albion.

3. It has four race courses: Randwick, Rosehill, Canterbury and Warwick Farm.

4. The nearby Royal National Park is the oldest national park in the world.

5. The oldest part of this city is known as the 'Rocks'.

6. It hosts a gay Mardi Gras every February.

7. At one time, the inhabitants of the city were predominately Anglo-Irish, but now it's a truly multi-national place, with more Maltese people than Malta itself.

8. The city's famous suspension bridge is known as the 'Coathanger'.

9. It has many similarities with London, including a park called Hyde Park.

0. An incredible shell-like Opera House stands in the harbour.

No ~ 10

Rare Roman wall paintings were discovered near here at The Forum of Jupiter.

An observatory was erected here in 1841-1845.

The wine that is produced here is called Lacrima Christi.

Pliny wrote of it, "Darkness fell as if a lamp had been put out in a closed room".

A dangerous year to have visited this place would have been 1944.

It is located inside Mount Summa.

Violent eruptions have occurred here since 79 AD.

It can be seen from Naples.

The town of Pompeii is at the foot of this mountain.

It is the only active volcano on the European mainland.

1

2

3

4

5

6

7

8

9

10

No ~ 11

This country is famous as a playground of the rich and famous.

Its merchant navy consists of one oil tanker.

Land has been reclaimed from the sea to extend the area available for commercial development.

The state has no army; it just has a Royal Guard of less than 100 men.

The late Formula One driver Ayrton Senna won the Grand Prix here six times.

Around 3% of the state revenue comes from casino royalties.

It is the second smallest independent state in the world.

It has been ruled by the Grimaldi family since the late 13th century.

Natives are known as Monégasques.

The late actress Grace Kelly was married to the reigning monarch.

No ~ 12

1. This constitutional monarchy comprises nine volcanic islands, only four of which are populated.

2. The Dutch explorer Jacob Roggeveen was the first European to visit the islands in 1722.

3. America has an overseas territory of the same name, less than a hundred miles further east.

4. In 1889, six battleships were sunk in the capital city's harbour during a typhoon.

5. The government relies on the village 'matai' system of law enforcement.

6. Its best-known export is Valima beer.

7. Robert Louis Stevenson died here.

8. The majority of inhabitants are Polynesian.

9. Situated in the South Pacific, it used to be administered by New Zealand but gained independence in 1962.

10. The national sport is Kirikiti, a bizarre form of cricket, and the country has a successful international rugby team.

No ~ 13

This capital city was formerly known as Kantipur.

It is located at the confluence of the Bishanmati and Bagmatti rivers.

It was founded by King Guanakamadeva in the 10th century.

It is home to 2,000 temples and religious shrines.

In 1934, it was destroyed by an earthquake.

There are more than 50 Buddhist monasteries, yet the official religion is Hinduism.

Houses in the city are typically brick-tiled with wooden balconies overhanging the crowded, narrow streets.

A goddess, known as Kumari, bestows authority on the King.

Durbar Square is the spiritual heart of the city.

It is situated on the ancient pilgrim and trade route from India to Tibet and China.

No ~ 14

This country was occupied by the Japanese during World War II.

It has the world's highest rate of widows and orphans.

Deforestation is one of its most serious environmental problems.

No comprehensive geological survey has ever been made of this country.

It gained independence as a constitutional monarchy under King Norodom Sihanouk in 1953.

More than half the country is covered by monsoon rainforest.

The temples of Angkor, built between the 7th and 11th centuries, are a popular tourist destination.

The Mekong River flows through this country.

The activities of Pol Pot's Khmer Rouge caused Vietnam to invade the country in 1978.

It was formerly known as Kampuchea.

No ~ 15

1. This city was founded by the Gauls almost 600 years BC.

2. After Austrian rule, Napoleon made it the capital of the Cisalpine Republic in 1797.

3. Despite being an ancient and historic city, its two universities date back to only the 1920s.

4. This colourful city houses the country's largest gay community.

5. The city boasts the fourth largest church in the world.

6. It is the commercial centre of Europe's silk trade.

7. It is the business, commercial and financial heart of the country.

8. Leonardo da Vinci painted the 'Last Supper' fresco in this city.

9. The 'Galleria Vittorio Emanuele II' is a shopper's Mecca.

10. Opera lovers can visit 'La Scala'.

No ~ 16

This city received its present name when captured by the English in 1664.

There is more than 26,000 acres of parkland in this city.

Its busy airport is named after a mayor who was in office from 1934-1945 and was nicknamed 'The Little Flower'.

The Gothic revivalist Trinity Church can be found in this city's financial district.

John Lennon was assassinated here in 1980.

It is named after an English duke.

The headquarters of the UN stretch along the East River.

The Giants and Jets do battle here.

The city was once called 'New Amsterdam'.

There is a giant green statue of a women holding a torch in the harbour.

No~17

This capital city started life as a town in the late 14th century.

It was the residence of the Masovian dukes until 1526.

Chopin gave one of his earliest performances here aged six.

In the past the city has fallen to the Swedes and the Russians.

Its civic symbol is a mermaid with a sword and shield.

Most of the city's historic buildings can be found along the Royal Axis.

Two thirds of the city's population were either dead or missing by the end of World War II.

It sits on the banks of the River Vistula.

A car park now stands on what was Europe's largest ghetto.

Eight former Eastern European countries signed a treaty, named after this city, on 14 May 1955 in reaction to the rearmament of the West by NATO.

No ~ 18

1 Indonesian settlers arrived in this country in the 1st century.

2 It is sometimes referred to as 'The Land of Thirst'.

3 The Hedgehog Tenrec is native to this country.

4 A French colony until 1896, the republic gained independence in 1960.

5 Habitats of the country's flora and fauna are threatened by the rapid development of forestry and soil erosion.

6 The capital city is Antananarivo.

7 It is the fourth largest island in the world.

8 Coffee, vanilla, cloves and sugar are the country's main products.

9 The main language is Malagasy.

10 The island lies off the coast of Mozambique.

No ~ 19

This city was settled in 1829 by Captain James Stirling.

The film "The Name of the Rose" was filmed 132km north of the city in an area called 'New Norcia'.

The 'Northbridge' area of the city is famed for its nightlife and excellent restaurants.

Its first flour mill is now a pioneer museum.

The city grew rapidly in the 1980s due to the rich mineral wealth of the area.

A wind, known as the 'Doctor', blows over the city from the sea.

Rupert Murdoch's media empire was founded here.

It is famous for its black swans.

The city was slow to develop until gold was discovered in the late 19th century.

A state capital, it is the fourth largest city in Australia.

1
2
3
4
5
6
7
8
9
1

No ~ 20

On 27 March 1964 a violent earthquake struck this area, killing 115 people and causing millions of dollars worth of damage.

The land was known as 'Seward's Folly', after the man who negotiated its purchase.

The first European to visit this place gave his name to the sea that lies off its west coast.

Nicknames for this area include The Land of the Midnight Sun, The Great Land and The Last Frontier.

The area is bisected from north to south by an 800 mile petroleum pipeline from Prudhoe Bay to Valdez.

The first salmon canneries were built here in 1878.

The breathtaking beauty of Denali National Park has made the area a major holiday destination.

The capital city is a huge urban sprawl, totally at odds with the vast tracts of unspoilt land that surround it.

It was bought from Russia for $7.2 million (2 cents per acre).

The area is the largest, and the 49th, of its kind.

No ~ 21

This city was of great strategic importance in the Middle Ages, when the country was at war with its neighbour.

The city suffered five earthquakes during September and October 1996, the strongest of which measured 2 on the Richter Scale.

The university, which dates from 1583, has a famous medical faculty.

There are monuments to Admiral Nelson and the defeat of Napoleon at Waterloo as well as statues of Allan Ramsay, William Pitt and the Duke of Wellington.

The writer James Boswell and philosopher David Hume were both sons of this city.

Giles Cathedral, which was built in 1385, is one of the city's landmarks.

High above the city, nestling on basalt cliffs, stands the old town and the city's historic 11th century castle.

The Commonwealth Games were held here in 1970 and 1986.

The city hosts an annual military tattoo.

Since 1947, thousands of thespians have flocked to this city for its annual international festival.

No ~ 22

Francisco de Orellana was the first European to travel in the area in 1542.

More than 150 different tribes, all of which speak a different language or dialect, live here.

It transgresses more than one country.

Around 15% of all the world's fresh water flows through here.

Red Piranha swim here.

More than two-thirds of the world's river water is to be found here.

It covers an area of 4,010 miles.

The Rio Negro, which joins this place, is so called because of the rotting vegetation that lies in the swamps where it gets much of its water.

Much of the jungle that surrounds this river was destroyed during the 1970s and 1980s.

It is the second longest river in the world.

This country's origins can be traced back to 110 BC.

It has been invaded many times by its large and powerful northerly neighbour.

The major religions of this country have developed into 'Tam Giao'.

The southern part of this country was conquered by the French in 1867.

A range of mountains and highlands called The Annamite Cordillera covers 75% of the country.

The currency is the dong.

It has two extensive river deltas; the Song Hong in the north and the Mekong in the south.

As well as the official language, Chinese, English, French, Khmer and Malayo-Polynesian are spoken.

Ho Chi Minh's forces defeated the French at Dien Bien Phu in 1954.

The war between the Communist north and American-backed south ended when Saigon fell to the Communist forces in 1975.

No~24

Gambling and prostitution are legal here.

Its name means 'snow-covered peaks'.

American nuclear testing is carried out here.

Nicknames for this place include Sagebush and the Silver and Battlehorn State.

It has more than 200 ghost towns, including Aurora, Eureka, Gold Hill and Rawhide.

Its main river is the Humboldt.

It is home to the highest dam is the USA.

It is the seventh largest US state.

It is situated next to California, Oregon, Idaho, Utah and Arizona.

Its capital is Carson City.

No ~ 25

Inhabitants can cross the river which flows through this capital city by boat, tunnel or bridge.

It was flooded in 1236, 1663, 1928 and 1953.

It is the seat of the country's royal family, its parliament, its central government and its highest courts of justice.

King Canute was the first monarch to have a palace here.

Dr Johnson said that when man is tired of this city, he is tired of life.

The set Virginia Woolf mixed with is named after part of this city.

For two days every year, the city is host to a street carnival, second in size only to Rio.

A tower built by William I is a famous city landmark.

Its financial centre is known as the 'square mile'.

Much of the city was destroyed by the great fire of 1666.

1
2
3
4
5
6
7
8
9
10

No ~ 26

The cities in this country originated as monasteries.

The country has one of the lowest population densities in the world - one person per square km.

The main form of transport in rural areas is horse and camel.

The traditional nomadic peoples of this country live in circular tents known as 'gers' or 'yurts'.

The staple drink is 'ayrag', which is made from fermented mare's milk.

It was once the centre of a great Eurasian Empire.

The main religion is Shamanist.

Its capital city is Ulan Bator.

You can visit the vast and arid Gobi Desert in the south of this country.

The inhabitants are descendants of Ghengis Khan.

This country was a German colony until World War I, after which it was divided between France and the UK.

The Oti River runs through this country.

The people in the south of this country speak Kwa languages and those in the north speak Voltaic languages.

Main agricultural crops include maize, cassava, yams, groundnuts and plantains.

It used to form part of what was once called the Slave Coast.

Around 20% of females in this country undergo circumcision.

Its first president was called Sylvanus Olympio.

The British part of the country was incorporated into Ghana, the present day country consists of the French half.

Neighbours include Berkina Faso and Benin.

The capital city hosted a meeting which resulted in the signing of the Lomé Convention, which gave third world countries in Africa, the Caribbean and the Pacific preferential treatment from the EU.

No ~ 28

This monarchy was a UK protectorate from 1888 and only gained independence in 1984.

It has a population of only 266,000.

There is a Winston Churchill Memorial Museum here.

In the 14th century it was a dependency of the Javanese Kingdom of Majapahit.

The head of state is Hassanal Bolkiah Muizzaddin Waddaulah.

The government bought a cattle station in Australia's Northern Territory to supply the country with beef, which is flown in daily. The cattle station is larger than the country which owns it.

Its ruler owns 200 Argentine polo ponies, which live in air-conditioned stables.

Education and healthcare in this Islamic Sultanate are free. Houses, cars and even pilgrimages to Mecca are subsidised by the state.

It is situated on the island of Borneo.

The country is divided in two by Sarawak.

No ~ 29

Its name comes from the soothsayers who used to live on the hill on which this sovereignty was built.

The tombs beneath the city include that of St Peter.

Its palace is one of the largest in the world and houses a highly valuable art collection.

Michelangelo spent four years painting the ceiling of a chapel here.

It is the destination of pilgrims from all over the world.

The city has an army of around 100 Swiss guards.

Entrance to the city is through St Peter's Church.

It is the world's smallest independent state.

It has a population of only 1,000 people.

The Pope is the sovereign.

No ~ 30

1 Originally a fishing village, the patronage of the Prince Regent helped turn this town into a thriving bathing resort.

2 The old town consists of many winding, narrow lanes, where the fishermen used to live, which are now famous for their antique and jewellery shops.

3 Thackeray, Arnold Bennett and Graham Greene have all written about it.

4 It boasts a pebble beach.

5 Its marina was re-built in 1979.

6 Architect John Nash worked on one of the town's most famous buildings.

7 The waterfront boasts twin piers, the Palace Pier, and its crumbling counterpart, the West Pier.

8 The town is home to Sussex University.

9 The town's Grand Hotel was once bombed by the IRA.

0 It acquired its present name in the 19th century; it was previously a village called Brighthelmstone.

No ~ 31

The Guanajatabeyes, the Ciboneys and the Arawaks were some of this country's earliest inhabitants.

The first European explorer to come here believed he was in Japan.

The country gained independence from Spain in 1898.

The local religion is 'Santeria', a synthesis of Catholicism & African beliefs.

It consists of one large island and over 1,500 smaller ones.

Tobacco is one of the country's main exports.

Slavery was abolished here in 1880.

Ernest Hemingway, Jean Paul Sartre and Graham Greene visited this country.

Being a communist state, most trading is done with the former USSR and former COMECON countries.

Relations between the country and the USA have been tense, especially during the Missile Crisis of 1962.

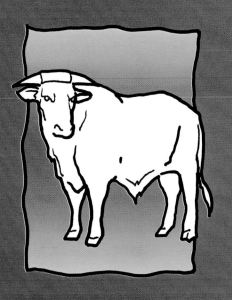

No ~ 32

This capital city was built on seven hills.

It was almost totally destroyed by a huge tidal wave and an earthquake in 1755.

It was founded by Phoenicians, who called it Alis Ubbo (Delightful Harbour).

It was the European terminal for the first scheduled transatlantic plane service, the Pan-American 'Clippers'.

The famous glass-house, the 'Estufa Fria', can be found in this city.

The 'Ponte 25 de Abril' is said to be the largest suspension bridge in Europe.

Bullfights are held at the principal 'Campo Pequeno' bullring.

It was from here that the explorer Vasco da Gama set sail for India.

It is the second most southerly capital in Europe.

A giant statue of Christ, with arms outstretched, looks down on the city.

No ~ 33

1. This city is the capital of a land-locked Asian country.

2. It is situated between the valleys of Chardeh and Koh Daman.

3. The emperor Baber wrote of the city as having "a scenery of mountains and valleys, wilderness and gardens so beautiful that the realisation of this beauty completely satisfies human taste".

4. The British fought three wars here between 1838 and 1919.

5. Rudyard Kipling wrote a poem about this place.

6. Life expectancy - 43 years for men and 41 for women - is very low.

7. There is a river of the same name which has its source in the Paghman mountains about 50m west of this city.

8. Pushtu and Dari are the languages spoken.

9. The city has been almost totally destroyed in a series of civil wars.

10. It controls the strategic route into Pakistan via the Khyber Pass.

No ~ 34

This capital city was established about 750 years ago.

Authorities are spending thousands of pounds on pigeon contraceptives in order to control the city's bird population.

Although Paris has twice the population, it could fit six times over in this enormous city.

The English playwright and novelist Christopher Isherwood recorded this city's decadence in the 1930s.

In the 13th century, it played a major part in the Hanseatic League.

It was once known as Cölln.

One of its most famous venues is a kitsch drag club called 'Chez Nous'.

The majority of the city has been rebuilt since 1945.

The city, which incorporates areas known as Spandau and Schöneberg, feels more like a collection of towns than a city.

In 1990, when the 'Wall' came down, the two parts of this city were reunited.

No ~ 35

This country was once a part of the Turkish Empire.

Natives call it Shqiperia, the land of the Eagles.

Its last Monarch was King Zog I.

The national hero is Gjergi Skanderbeg, who started a rebellion against the Turks in 1442.

Inhabitants are descended from the ancient Illyrians.

The two languages spoken are Task and Geg.

It was invaded by Mussolini in 1939 and used as a springboard for his invasion of Greece in October 1940.

The national drink is raki.

It was a communist republic from 1944-1990.

It is one of the Balkan states, situated on the eastern seaboard of the Adriatic Sea.

No ~ 36

A Spanish colony since 1565, this country ceded to the US in 1898 and gained independence in 1946.

In the first four months of 1996, 55 people - mostly businessmen - were kidnapped in this country.

Local specialities include kneecap soup and offal and sour vegetable broth.

Main cities include Davao, Cebu, Bacolod and Zamboanga.

The official language is based on 'Tagalog'.

The republic has been battered and bruised by many typhoons.

The capital gets its name from the bay on which it stands.

It is an archipelago comprising three main island groups.

This is the only Christian country in the whole of Asia.

A former first lady was famed for her enormous shoe collection.

No ~ 37

This is the capital city of a country which is divided into two parts.

It suffered severe earthquakes in 1848, 1855 and 1942.

It was founded in 1840 by Edward Gibbon Wakefield.

A cable car runs the 400ft journey from Lambton Quay to Kelburn.

Its government building is one of the world's largest wooden structures and is known as 'the beehive'.

The city was named after Arthur Wellesley.

It is known as the 'windy city', because of the constant west winds.

The site was settled by Maoris around the 12th century.

The harbour is called Port Nicholson.

It is situated in Cook Strait.

1

2

3

4

5

6

7

8

9

10

No ~ 38

This republic gained independence in 1991.

It has a coastline on the Sea of Azov.

Ulysses took refuge here, in the Bay of Balaklava.

The River Dneiper runs through the country.

The Pecherskaya Lavra (Monastery of the Caves), which incorporates churches, tombs and monuments, is here.

Borscht is one of the national dishes.

Dessert wines are produced in the south of this country in the Crimea.

Its seaport of Odessa is known as 'the pearl of the Black Sea'.

It was formerly part of the USSR.

A nuclear reactor at Chernobyl exploded here in 1986.

No ~ 39

1 This region is over 15,000 years old.

2 Captain Cook stumbled upon it by accident in 1770.

3 It is 1,250 miles long.

4 It is not uncommon to see sharks here.

5 Human sweat is one of the many things that threatens its well being.

6 It has a major natural enemy in the 'Crown of Thorns Starfish'.

7 It is home to over 2,000 species of fish, great whales and beautiful corals.

8 Hard corals release their spores after the November full moon, turning the sea pink.

9 This is the largest structure in the world to be built by a living organism.

10 It is close to the Australian coastline.

No ~ 40

This capital city is one of the oldest continually inhabited cities in the world.

It is situated on the banks of the River Barada.

It was founded by Uz, son of Aram.

There are more than 30 mosques here, including the Ommiad Mosque, which towers over the city.

The old city was rectangular in shape and surrounded by a wall with seven gates.

The head of John the Baptist is said to be buried in this city.

It is connected to the seaport of Beirut by a narrow-gauge railroad.

It is mentioned twice in the book of Genesis in the Bible.

St Paul received his calling on the road to this city.

The Arab name for this city is Dimashq.

1
2
3
4
5
6
7
8
9
10

No ~ 41

Seven states in America have a place of the same name as this capital city.

It dates back to the 3rd century BC.

It used to be the capital city of the ancient kingdom of Attica.

One of the city's most famous landmarks was destroyed in 1687 by Venetian forces besieging the Turks.

Lord Byron once said of this city, "Shrine of the mighty! Can it be that this is all that remains of thee?".

Its population has quadrupled in the past 40 years, and now makes up a third of the country's population.

Steeped in history and once famed as an oasis of peace and beauty, this city now has dire noise and air pollution problems.

You can get a meal here in an estiatorio, a taverna or a psistaria.

Piraeus is the name of the city's busy port.

Aristotle, Plato and Socrates are just some of the intellectuals linked to the city.

No ~ 42

1 By the 5th century, the Romans had been driven out of this country by the Alemanni.

2 Frankenstein was written by Mary Shelley in this country.

3 It has four official languages including Romansch.

4 Its Roman name, which appears on its stamps, is Helvetia.

5 Goethe described it as a happy mix of 'the colossal and the well-ordered'.

6 Only in 1971, were women given the right to vote and run for office in federal elections.

7 It has won more Nobel prizes per head than any other country.

8 Its national dish is made with cheese, wine and kirsch.

9 It is famed for the cuckoo clock, despite it being a German invention.

10 This mountainous country is a financial haven.

No ~ 43

The country's main industries are food processing and metals.

Infant mortality here is very high - 98 per 1,000 children born.

Animals found here include deer, boars, bears, wolves, jackals and hyenas.

It gained independence in 1947.

Basmati rice is grown in the Sind region of this country.

The landscape and economy is dominated by the River Indus and its tributaries.

Visitors travel to this country to climb K2, the second highest mountain in the world.

The fearsome Pashtan tribe lives in the north west of this country.

A Federal Islamic Republic, it separated from Bangladesh in 1971.

Cricket is the national sport and Imran Khan a local hero.

No ~ 44

The name of this capital city means 'Dark Pool'.

Danish invaders first established themselves here in 840 AD.

It is a seaport, a market town and an Episcopal see.

Handel directed his Messiah in this city's famous music hall on 13 April 1742.

When Jonathan Swift died, he left money to build a lunatic asylum in this city.

Its university was founded by Queen Elizabeth I.

It was the birth place of WB Yeats, James Joyce and George Bernard Shaw.

In 1682, 1,200 of the 6,025 buildings in the city were pubs.

It is situated on the River Liffey.

It is the home of Molly Malone from the folk song "Cockles and Mussels".

No ~ 45

1 This country is now a kingdom but in the past it has been ruled by the Romans, the French, the Spanish and, in part, by the Portuguese.

2 Half the population is under 20 years of age.

3 There are 12 times as many cows here as there are human beings.

4 Arabic is the official language, but French is also understood.

5 This country's main Atlantic port was made famous by Humphrey Bogart and Ingrid Bergman in a film named after the city.

6 It is part of the Magreb region of Africa.

7 Men wear the red, tasselled pill-box hats, named after one of the country's main cities.

8 Algeria and the Western Sahara border this country.

9 Visitors can climb the Atlas Mountains.

0 The Rock of Gibraltar can be seen from the country's most northern port.

No ~ 46

This country used to be entirely inhabited by nomadic tribes.

Its capital city remained of little importance for almost two centuries after its establishment.

The country is home to many rare and exotic birds, including the rhea and the condor.

The revolutionary Che Guevara was born here on 14 June 1928.

It gained independence from Spain in 1816.

It is the eighth largest country in the world.

It shares an island territory with Chile.

During the so-called 'Dirty War' thousands of people simply 'disappeared'.

It is renowned for its huge cattle ranches.

The 'Islas Malvinas' are just off its coast.

No ~ 47

This city was an important centre of commerce when ruled by the Roman Empire and then by the British between the 12th and 15th centuries.

It was the temporary seat of the government in 1870, 1914 and 1940.

It used to be the capital of the Celtic Vivisci tribe and in Roman Times it flourished under the name of Burdigala.

The city is the capital of one of the world's largest wine growing areas.

It sits on the banks of the River Garonne.

It is close to the Bay of Biscay.

Jacques Chirac was once mayor of this city.

It is a short trip down the coast to the famous seaside resort of Biarritz.

It is the home of claret.

A literal translation of the city's name is 'by the waters'.

No ~ 48

This city is one of the largest in a country in which hydroelectricity plays a major power role.

It takes its name from a small mountain named by Jacques Cartier, who claimed it for the King of France in 1535.

Alfa Romeo produced a special edition car, named after the city, which hosted the 1967 World Expo.

The city is noted for its many churches and religious buildings like the Gothic Church of Notre Dame and The Place D'Armes.

The oldest building in the city, St Sulpice Seminary, was built in 1685.

It was captured by the British in 1760.

The Olympic Games were held here in 1976.

This is the 2nd largest French-speaking city in the world.

It boasts two English-speaking and two French-speaking universities.

It lies on the banks of the St Lawrence River.

No ~ 49

This country was discovered in the 15th century by Vasco da Gama.

The natives are of Bantu origin.

It was a Portuguese colony until it gained independence in 1975.

The Frelimo resistance party was responsible for the expulsion of the Portuguese.

Tourists were banned from entering the country in 1975.

President Machel was killed in a mysterious plane crash just over the South African border on 19 October 1986.

It has a wide and varied wildlife, which is protected in reserves and national parks, the most famous of which is the Gorongosa.

The capital city was formerly known as Lorenco Marques.

Numerous rivers like the Zambesi and the Limpopo cross the country.

It shares a border with Tanzania, Malawi, Zambia, Zimbabwe, South Africa and Swaziland.

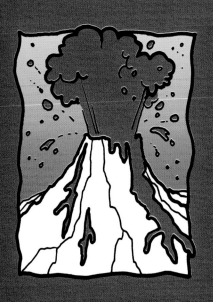

No ~ 50

The first inhabitants of this place arrived here around 500 AD.

Less than 1% of the total population still speak the native language.

The first European to arrive here was believed to be the God of fertility and peace, but it didn't save him from being stabbed to death by native savages.

In the 1830s it was an important whaling centre.

Mark Twain said it must be, "the loveliest fleet of islands that lies anchored in any ocean".

One of its main economic assets is tourism.

The largest of the islands is home to the active Volcano Kilauea.

These islands were once known as The Sandwich Islands.

Windsurfers enjoy the swells off Maui and Oahu.

The kingdom became a republic in 1893, then an American annex and finally in 1959, the 50th US state.

No ~ 51

1 Marco Polo was the first European to reach this country in 1290.

2 It has the world's largest Muslim population.

3 It is made up of more than 13,000 islands, 3,000 of which are uninhabited.

4 It was occupied by the Japanese from 1942-45.

5 Boats carry enormous symbolic importance in this country.

6 There are 200 indigenous languages.

7 The islands are situated in the Celebes, Flores, Banda and Arafura Seas.

8 Natives use the batik method of wax-dying to produce patterned textiles such as traditional sarongs.

9 Sumatra, Irian Jaya, Timor, Bali, Kalimantan and Halmahera are some of the islands, known as the 'Spice Islands'.

10 It was once known as the Dutch East Indies.

No ~ 52

The summer palace, just outside this capital city, is built in the shape of a Star of David.

The city is known as 'The Golden City'.

It was referred to in 965 AD by the Arab merchant Ibrahim as the "town built of stone and lime".

12 bridges connect the west bank of the city to the east bank, where the greater part of the city lies.

It was one of the few European cities to escape bombing by either the Nazis or the Allies during World War II.

The Hapsburgs ruled this city during the 16th century.

Charles University, which dates from 1348, is the oldest university in Central Europe.

The national saint, St Wenceslas, is interred in St Vitus' Cathedral.

Glass engraving was developed here by Caspar Lehmann for Rudolph II.

It is the capital city of a republic which separated from Slovakia in 1993.

1
2
3
4
5
6
7
8
9

No ~ 53

This country is rich in bauxite.

The Arawak Indians once inhabited the island, but were exterminated by the Spanish.

It was named Santiago by Columbus, after the patron saint of Spain.

The island is situated in the centre of the Greater Antilles chain of islands in the Caribbean Sea.

About two-thirds of the country is a limestone plateau more than 3,000 feet above sea level.

A British colony since 1670, the country gained independence in 1962.

Errol Flynn and Ginger Rogers visited the island.

It was once a central player in the slave trade.

'Jerk chicken' is a local speciality.

Bob Marley called this country home.

No ~ 54

1. This capital city was established on the site of a citadel built by Vlad the Impaler.

2. It was founded in the 18th century by Radel the Black of Wallachia.

3. Its name means 'City of Joy'.

4. It has a Triumphal Arch built in 1935-36, modelled on the Parisian Arc de Triomphe, and is known as 'the little Paris of the east'.

5. An earthquake in 1977 caused considerable damage to this city.

6. A treaty was signed here on 10 August 1913 ending the second Balkan War.

7. The Germans occupied the city during both World Wars.

8. The Royal Palace was badly damaged by Axis bombers during World War II.

9. It is situated on the River Dîmbovitza.

10. Much of the old city was demolished on Ceausescu's orders, to create a civic centre worthy of 'the capital of the new socialist man'.

The country's first inhabitants were Irish Monks, who lived here around the 9th century.

It has the oldest parliament in the world.

Although officially a Christian country, the native beliefs of the Asatrú are gaining popularity.

Local specialities include pickled ram's testicle cake, singed sheep's head and decomposed shark meat.

The country has the highest birth rate in Europe yet it has a population density of only two people per square km.

The capital city is known to the locals as 'The Smokey City'.

Its main power source is geothermal.

The landscape is entirely volcanic with substantial ice sheets, lava fields, still-active volcanoes, geysers and hot springs.

There is just one indigenous land animal here, the Arctic Fox.

The British were once prominent here, but the 'Cod War' in the 1970s changed that.

No ~ 56

This city is known as I'Goli, the city of gold.

It is home to a fine art gallery that Sir Edwin Lutyens designed in 1911.

The affluent parts of the city are counter-balanced by its poverty-ridden suburbs.

The city's airport is named after a former prime minister.

More than 100 people died here during the student riots of 1976.

It is the third largest city in Africa.

It has two major communications towers - the JG Strijdom Tower and The Brixton Tower - to the north of the city centre.

Settlement began here in the 1880s, following the discovery of gold at the ridge of white waters.

The city hosts Africa's only Lesbian and Gay Pride march.

Although it is the country's economic heart, it is not one of the country's three capital cities.

No ~ 57

1 This country achieved independence from Britain in 1971.

2 It is an absolute monarchy.

3 It was part of the Ottoman Empire from 1827 until World War II.

4 More than 40% of the country's GNP is spent on defence.

5 Only one in five of its inhabitants were born in the country.

6 Its main source of revenue is from the exploitation of its vast oil and gas reserves.

7 From 1980-1988, it backed Iraq in its war against Iran.

8 It was a founder member of OPEC.

9 During the Gulf War in 1991, it helped the US-led forces drive Iraq out of Kuwait.

10 A flat, dry, desert peninsula, it reaches north into The Gulf from north-east Saudi Arabia.

No ~ 58

Documents have been found tracing this kingdom's history back to the Middle Ages, but it was inhabited many centuries before then.

A Lutheran country, Christianity only got a foothold here around the 12th century, before then pagan deities were worshipped.

The country's capital city is built on a series of 14 small islands.

In 1995, this country had a higher proportion of pensioners in its population than any other country in the world.

Wolves, bears, lynx and wolverines can be found in the countryside.

The top of Mount Kebnekaise is the highest point in the country.

Alcohol is bought from the state run 'Systembolaget', which has outlets in almost every town.

One of this country's most famous sons was Alfred Nobel, founder and patron of the Nobel Peace Prize.

National dishes include Gravadlax, Fruksoppa and Smörgasbord.

This country gave the world ABBA, Volvo cars, Greta Garbo and Britt Ekland.

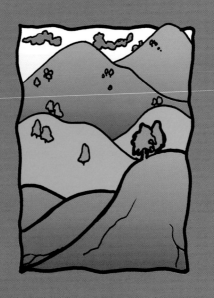

No ~ 59

This city was built on seven hills.

It stands on the site of the ancient city of Byzantium.

It was once the capital city of the Ottoman Empire.

The Covered Bazaar, which dates from the 15th century, is a maze of narrow, winding streets and thousands of small shops.

The Golden Gate, the Gate of Selviria and the Gate of St Romanus can all be found in the ancient city walls.

One of its suburbs is called Scutari, where Florence Nightingale nursed the wounded during the Crimean War.

The Topkapi Palace, originally the Sultan's residence, is now a museum complex.

The city's 17th century Mosque of Sultan Ahmed is called the Blue Mosque after the colour of its beautiful interior tiles.

Its natural harbour is known as the Golden Horn.

Situated on the Bosphorus, it was once known as Constantinople.

No ~ 60

1. This republic was a constituent part of the USSR until 1991.

2. Known as 'the sunny republic', it makes extensive use of hydro-electric power.

3. National dishes include Shashlik (skewered lamb) and Plov (Pilau rice), supposedly invented by Alexander the Great.

4. The region was part of some very old Persian states, including Khorezm and Sogdiana.

5. There are more police per square mile than anywhere else in Central Asia.

6. It is situated on the Silk Road from Europe to China.

7. It is located between Central Asia's two largest rivers; the Syr Darya in the north and the Amu Darya in the south.

8. It was once part of Ghengis Khan's Mongol Empire.

9. Neighbours include Kazakhstan, Turkmenistan, Kirghizia and Tajikistan.

10. The name of the capital city, Tashkent, means 'stone village'.

No ~ 61

Founded in the 3rd century, parts of this capital city's earliest settlements date back to Roman times.

Street urchins are known locally as 'Titi'.

A treaty signed here on 3 September 1783 ended the War of American Independence.

Its Roman name is 'Lutetia'.

Oscar Wilde, Amedeo Modigliani and Jim Morrison are buried here.

It features in Charles Dickens' "A Tale of Two Cities".

UNESCO is one of the many international organisations based here.

The city has the same name as the son of Priam and Hecuba.

One of the city's foremost landmarks is a tower, built for the Exposition of 1889 and named after its architect.

Napoleon had a major effect on the city's architecture, commissioning many beautiful buildings.

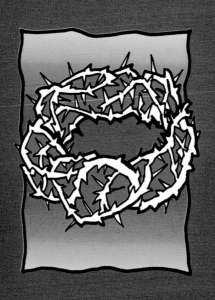

No ~ 62

This country was invaded by the Aztecs and the Spanish.

It was discovered by Pedro de Alvarado in 1524.

Its highest mountains, Santa Ana and San Vincente, are both volcanoes.

Only 50 miles wide, its coastline stretches more than three times this distance.

A civil war in the 1980s and early 1990s drove more than 1 million refugees into exile.

Its principal river is the Rio Lempa.

It is the smallest and most densely populated country in Latin America.

The Pan American Highway runs the entire length of the country.

It was part of Guatemala until 1821.

It is named after the saviour Jesus Christ.

No ~ 63

This country is two-thirds mountain or desert.

It came into existence in its present form in 1949.

A cultural revolution took place in 1966.

An army of terracotta soldiers is buried in this country.

It is home to the only man-made structure visible from space.

The Huang He River, which is 3,208 miles long, is also known as The Yellow River.

Its capital houses the Forbidden City.

In 1989 between 1,000 and 2,000 unarmed pro-democracy protesters were massacred in the Square of Heavenly Peace.

One in five of the world's population live in this people's republic.

It is bordered by Mongolia, Tajikistan, Kyrgystan, Afghanistan, India, Nepal, Bhutan, Myanmar, Laos, Vietnam, Russia and North Korea.

No ~ 64

Every Jew was expelled from this country in 1492.

In 1931, the King abdicated and the Second Republic was formed.

Europe's only desert can be found in this country.

A Civil War was waged from 1936-39.

The Olympic Games were held here in 1992.

It is known to the Berbers as Al-Andalus (The isle of the Vandals).

Nougat comes from the area of this country once occupied by the Moors.

The Canary and Balearic Islands are owned by this country.

It makes up four fifths of the Iberian Peninsula.

King Juan Carlos is currently on the throne.

No ~ 65

This country has been dominated by Phoenicia, Greece, Rome, Byzantium and the Ottoman empire.

It is made up of three former provinces of Tripolitania, Cyrenaica and the Fezzan.

Pliny described how the inhabitants, the Blemmyae, had faces in the middle of their chests.

The monarchy was overthrown and a republic declared in September 1969.

It was occupied by Italy from 1911-1912.

Alleged traitors and spies are publicly executed.

In 1970, all property belonging to Italians and Jews was confiscated.

More than 90% of its land area is desert.

On 15 April 1986, US aircraft bombed targets in this country.

The country's ruler is Muammar al Qaddafi.

Solutions

<u>Solutions</u>

1   Mexico City, Mexico
2   Tunis, Tunisia
3   Sri Lanka
4   Venice, Italy
5   Ecuador
6   Gibraltar
7   San Francisco, USA
8   Moscow, Russia
9   Sydney, Australia
10 Mount Vesuvius, Italy
11 Monaco
12 Western Samoa
13 Kathmandu, Nepal
14 Cambodia
15 Milan, Italy
16 New York, USA
17 Warsaw, Poland
18 Madagascar
19 Perth, Australia
20 Alaska, USA
21 Edinburgh, Scotland
22 River Amazon
23 Vietnam

Solutions

24   Nevada, USA

25   London, England

26   Mongolia

27   Togo

28   Brunei

29   Vatican City, Italy

30   Brighton, England

31   Cuba

32   Lisbon, Portugal

33   Kabul, Afghanistan

34   Berlin, Germany

35   Albania

36   Philippines

37   Wellington, New Zealand

38   Ukraine

39   Great Barrier Reef, Australia

40   Damascus, Syria

41   Athens, Greece

42   Switzerland

43   Pakistan

44   Dublin, Ireland

<u>**Solutions**</u>

45	Morocco
46	Argentina
47	Bordeaux, France
48	Montreal, Canada
49	Mozambique
50	Hawaii, USA
51	Indonesia
52	Prague, Czech Republic
53	Jamaica
54	Bucharest, Romania
55	Iceland
56	Johannesburg, S. Africa
57	Qatar
58	Sweden
59	Istanbul, Turkey
60	Uzbekistan
61	Paris, France
62	El Salvador
63	China
64	Spain
65	Libya